TALKING ABOUT

Alcohol

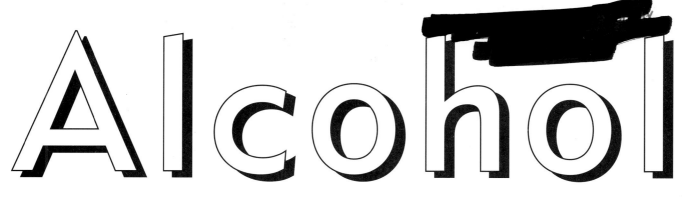

Sarah Levete

Franklin Watts
London • Sydney

© Aladdin Books Ltd 2004

Designed and produced by
Aladdin Books Ltd
28 Percy Street
London W1T 2BZ

First published in Great
Britain in 2004 by
Franklin Watts
96 Leonard Street
London EC2A 4XD

ISBN: 0 7496 5511 9

Design:
Flick, Book Design and
Graphics

Picture research:
Brian Hunter Smart

Editor:
Jim Pipe

The consultant, David
Uffindall, is a Drugs
Education Consultant with a
Local Education Authority.

The publishers would like
to acknowledge that the
photographs reproduced
in this book have been
posed by models or have
been obtained from
photographic agencies.

A CIP record for this book
is available from the
British Library.

Contents

"Why should I know about alcohol?"

You may wonder why you need to know about alcohol. After all, it is all around you. Supermarkets are stacked high with bottles and cans of alcoholic drinks. People drink alcohol in pubs and clubs. Your parents and teachers may drink at home, with friends or to celebrate. However, drinking too much or too often can badly damage a person's health or make them seriously ill.

Enjoying just one or two drinks can be fun, but for some, drinking alcohol is a real risk.

As you grow older, you will probably be offered an alcoholic drink at some point. This book helps you understand how alcohol might affect your body and your behaviour. It can make some people feel relaxed, but makes others violent.

If you know the risks, then you can make informed choices. Lots of people enjoy alcohol but avoid problems by drinking only a small amount. Many others choose not to drink for religious or health reasons, or just because they don't like the taste.

"What is alcohol?"

Alcohol is a drug. It changes the way a person behaves and thinks. It changes the normal way the body works.

The scientific name for alcohol is ethanol. This clear, colourless liquid is made when yeast and sugars react in a process called fermentation. The flavour and colour of a drink come from the ingredients used to make it.

From beer to alcopops, there are many different types and flavours of alcoholic drink.

For instance, wine is made from fermented grapes. Beer or lager is made by brewing barley or other fermented grains. Spirits such as gin and vodka are made in a process called distilling.

Did you know...

You may have seen a friend or relative lose control as they drink more and more. This is known as getting drunk. But how drunk someone gets also depends on his or her age, size, sex and what they are drinking.

It isn't always easy to tell how much alcohol is in something just by its taste. Some drinks, like alcopops (left), taste like soft drinks, even though they may contain more alcohol than beer. Cider may taste sweet but is a powerful alcoholic drink.

"What does alcohol do to the body?"

When someone drinks, alcohol passes through the stomach and travels around the body in the blood. It soon starts to change the way the body works. Alcohol stops a person from thinking clearly and relaxes the body, making a person sleepy. It switches off inhibitions – the natural fears that stop us from doing something foolish or risky.

Alcohol is a drug which slows down the mind and body.

Did you know...

Have you seen the effect of alcohol on someone you know? If they have drunk too much they may feel dizzy or find it hard to stand up straight. It may look funny but they have lost control. Their eyesight may become fuzzy or blurred. Alcohol slows down the brain's reactions. That is why drinking and driving is so dangerous.

Alcohol makes the brain lose control of balance and limbs. This is why someone who is drunk may fall over. The liver works hard to get rid of alcohol. But people are often ill if they drink too much, because the body cannot cope. The poisoning effect of alcohol can stay in the body for up to 12 hours or more. That's why people who have drunk too much have hangovers.

"How does alcohol make people behave?"

You may have heard people talking about the "buzz" they get from alcohol. A drink can make a person feel relaxed. But it can also make them feel sad or depressed. After a drink or two, people may also say things they wouldn't otherwise say. This can make them upset or embarrassed the next day. They may not even remember what happened.

Drinking can make problems seem unimportant. But it can also make them seem even worse.

When drunk, people can't think clearly. They are more likely to take risks or become aggressive, leading to fights.

However, lots of people enjoy alcohol without needing to get drunk. They take it easy by having a non-alcoholic (soft) drink between alcoholic drinks or by drinking smaller amounts.

My Story

"My brother's girlfriend is lovely but after a few drinks she changes into a really aggressive person. She starts picking fights with people around her, even her friends. My brother is mad about her but every time they go out he worries about what she will do." Roberta

"What are the risks of drinking alcohol?"

Drinking too much over a long period of time can seriously damage a person's body.

You may know many grown-ups who enjoy a few drinks without having any problems. That is probably because they understand the risks of drinking too much alcohol.

But when young people drink alcohol, they may not realise how quickly it can affect them. If they drink a lot in a short time, it can cause alcohol poisoning. This can make them seriously ill.

Regularly drinking too much can cause liver, heart and kidney problems. It can also lead to depression and mental health problems.

Some people drink so much they become dependent on alcohol. This means they may find it very hard to do anything without having a drink first.

Drinking while taking medicines can also lead to a very serious reaction. Mixing alcohol with illegal "street" drugs increases the risk of a drugs overdose.

Think about it

Lots of people drink alcohol. But there are more young people suffering from serious problems caused by alcohol abuse than by illegal drugs. Each year, over 1,000 children in England have to go to hospital suffering from alcohol poisoning and needing emergency treatment. Some even die.

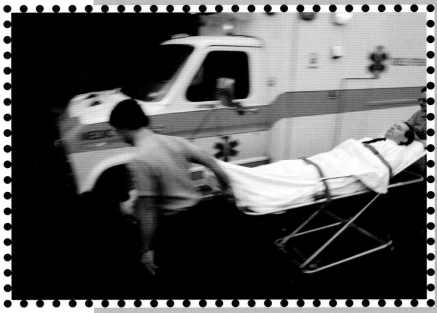

"Why do people drink?"

People often drink because it helps them relax and have a pleasant time with their family or friends.

Relaxing can make a person feel more confident, especially in situations such as meeting new people or going to a party.

However, drinking too much muddles a person's thinking and mood, so it can also make them feel hopeless and uncomfortable.

Many people enjoy the taste of beer or wine with a meal.

Some people drink because they want to feel more confident and be more attractive to their friends. But is it attractive to drink too much and be sick over the floor?

Many young people first try alcohol because they think drinking is "grown-up". Some start drinking because they have been told not to! Others drink because their friends do, and they don't want to seem uncool.

My story

"Some of my mates said getting drunk was a blast. At first I didn't like the taste and felt sick. But I kept doing it. It was a laugh. But then a friend nearly drowned in the canal when we'd been drinking. It scared me. I'm more careful about how much I drink now. I don't want to be out of it like that." Mark

"Does drinking make you look good?"

Some young people think drinking makes them look cool or grown-up, but have you ever watched a person who has had too much to drink? Do they look attractive and in control?

When people are drunk they often behave in an embarrassing or simply dangerous way. Sometimes they lose control, get sick, lie down to sleep and wake up with a horrible hangover.

Advertisements for alcohol never show the ugly side of drinking.

Think about it

Being drunk means losing control – and no one can look good when they don't even know what they are doing. It can lead to problems, such as stealing. People get into trouble with the police which may result in a criminal record. A growing number of young people also end up with injuries because of accidents that happen when they are drunk.

Adverts for alcoholic drinks often show happy, trendy people. They make it look as if drinking always makes people have fun and look good. But they don't show the unpleasant things that happen to people after drinking too much.

"Are there laws about alcohol?"

You may wonder why, if alcohol can be so dangerous, it is legal (allowed by law). Most countries already have laws about drinking (page 19). But some people believe there should be stricter laws, as there are for other drugs. Others believe that the way to stop problems linked to alcohol is for people to drink only a limited amount.

It is against the law to sell alcohol to children.

It is against the law to:

① Sell alcohol to anyone under the age of 18, except in certain circumstances. The minimum drinking age is 18 in Australia, 20 in New Zealand.

② Buy alcohol for anyone under the age of 18, except in certain situations.

③ Drink in the streets in some places. This is to prevent fights or crime that can happen when people are drunk.

④ Give alcohol to children under five, unless prescribed by a doctor.

⑤ Drive or operate machinery after drinking more than a certain amount.

My story

"My religion is Islam. We are not allowed to drink alcohol. Mum and Dad always have soft drinks at parties. They don't mind if other people drink but they don't want alcohol in the house. My elder brother's non-Muslim friends tried to persuade us to try a drink but we weren't interested. We know we can have fun without drinking."
Tariq

"Can people drink safely?"

You may think that laws just stop people from having fun. But they are there to protect you. Younger people cannot drink like adults because their bodies are less able to deal with alcohol. The best way for people to drink safely is to drink sensibly. This means:

① Thinking why they want an alcoholic drink. Can't they have fun without alcohol?

② Watching how much they drink. It helps to know how strong different drinks are.

Enjoying one or two drinks with a meal is a safe, sensible way to drink alcohol.

③ Eating beforehand to reduce the alcohol's effect.

④ Not mixing drinks such as wine and beer.

⑤ Choosing low alcohol drinks or drinking soft drinks in between alcoholic ones.

It also makes sense to drink in a safe place. You may have spotted teenagers drinking in secret places to avoid getting caught. But it is taking a risk to drink out-of-sight or near rivers or railways, where accidents are more likely.

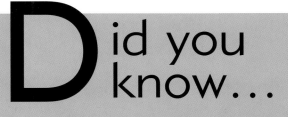id you know…

Some teenagers like the taste of cider or alcopops, but they may not realise how strong these drinks are. However, there are guidelines for working out how strong a drink is, based on units of alcohol. These tell people how much they are really drinking, so they can enjoy alcohol without any of the problems. This list shows the strength of different drinks in units:

- A glass of wine is 1-2 units.
- A pub measure of spirits, such as whisky or vodka, is 1 unit.
- A half pint of beer/ lager is 1 unit, but a can of strong lager is up to 3 units.
- A bottle of strong cider is 2 units.
- A bottle of alcopop can be 1.3 units or more.

If a man and woman drink the same amount, the effect will be greater on the woman, and even greater on a young teenager or a child.

"How can I say "no" to drinking?"

As you grow older, others may encourage you to drink. Never feel embarrassed if you don't want to drink. These tips will help you say "No" to alcohol and to feel okay about your choice:

① Stand tall, look directly at others and clearly say "No thanks." If you sound unsure, others will keep trying to persuade you.

There are lots of ways to have fun with your friends that don't involve alcohol.

② Choose friends who like you for who you are, whether or not you drink.

③ Avoid situations where others put pressure on you.

④ Trust your decision and be clear about it.

⑤ Build your confidence by getting involved in activities that make you feel good.

⑥ Just choose a soft drink – and enjoy being in control.

⑦ Ask advice from a grown-up you trust.

Think about it

It's hard to go against what friends do. But if you are offered a drink, think about the risks of drinking alcohol and how it could affect you. It is your decision, though it will also affect others around you, such as your friends and family.

If others make you feel uncomfortable because you choose not to drink, are they really the sort of people with whom you want to be friends?

"When is alcohol a problem?"

You may have heard young people boasting about how much they can drink. But drinking too much can quickly become a habit and then a problem, and often before the person realises it.

It can happen to anyone, at any age. Others may notice the problem if a person is often drunk, often misses school or work because of a hangover, or gets into trouble or fights when drunk.

Someone who needs a drink before doing any everyday task may well have an alcohol problem.

Did you know…

An alcoholic is a person who depends upon alcohol every day. He or she may spend lots of money on drink and may steal in order to pay for it. His or her behaviour may be so difficult and unpleasant when drunk that family life suffers and relationships break down.

A baby born to a woman who regularly drinks too much may be born with serious problems, and may even be born alcoholic.

A person may also have an alcohol problem if he or she thinks constantly about the next drink, needs a drink before going out, drinks secretly and lies about how much he or she has drunk.

They may need support to help them stop or cut back on drinking.

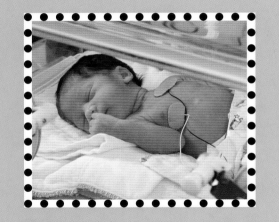

"Does alcohol affect others?"

Alcohol isn't just a problem for the person who drinks too much. If there is an alcoholic in your family you will know how upsetting it can be for family or friends.

Because people lose control when they are drunk, they are sometimes violent, even to those they love. They may say hurtful things that they later regret.

A loving parent may turn into a frightening person when drunk.

Drinking too much doesn't just create upset. It costs lots of money. Hospitals have to look after people suffering from alcohol poisoning or cuts from drunken falls or fights. The time and money spent doing this could be used to treat people suffering from serious injuries or illnesses.

Think about it

A person who drinks and drives not only puts their own life at risk – they put the lives of other people in danger as well. For instance, a child could be crossing the road carefully, but a drunk driver may not be able to see them clearly. If the driver cannot stop the car in time, they could kill the child.

"How can I help?"

If someone close to you has an alcohol problem, they may need help and support. The person with the drinking problem can choose to stop drinking, but others can help. If a family member has a drinking problem, tell a grown-up about your worries.

Sharing your worries with a grown-up doesn't mean you don't love the person involved.

If you have a friend who is becoming involved with drinking, talk to a grown-up you trust. They will be able to help find the support your friend needs.

If you feel under pressure to drink or already drink often without permission, talk to a grown-up you trust about what is going on.

My story

"My mum used to drink a lot during the day. It went on for a while. She was very unhappy, so I told my dad how worried I was about it. He understood and Mum and he had a chat. Mum started to go to some groups and it really made a difference. Now she's like my mum again!"
Wayne

"What about me?"

- If you are offered a drink, think. Drinking can result in poor school work or trouble with the police. It can make people very unwell.

- Be aware of the risks of drinking alcohol. They are much greater for young people as their body and mind are not fully developed. If you choose to drink alcohol when you are older, your body will be better able to cope with it.

- Stand up for yourself and for your right to say no to alcohol. Be proud of your decision not to drink and choose friends who like you for who you are, not for what you drink.

Enjoy the highs of life without the lows that come with drinking.

Books on alcohol

If you want to read more about alcohol, try:

The *My Healthy Body* series by
Jen Green (Franklin Watts)
Choices and Decisions: Drinking Alcohol by
Pete Sanders & Steve Myers (Franklin Watts)
Learn to say no: Alcohol
(Heinemann)

Contact information

If you want to talk to someone who doesn't
know you, these organisations can help:

Childline
Tel: 0800 1111
A 24-hour free helpline for children.

Drinkline
A national alcohol helpline providing
counselling, support, advice and information.
Helpline: 0800 917 8282, available 9am-11pm
Tuesday, Wednesday, Thursday and Friday.
9am until 11pm on Monday evenings

Support for Children Affected by Drink (SCAD)
A helpline for young people worried about
someone with an alcohol problem.
10 Sansome Place, Worcester WR1 1UA
Tel: 01905 23060, Helpline: 0800 318272

On the Web

These websites are also helpful:

www.childline.org.uk
www.wiredforhealth.gov.uk
www.galaxy-h.gov.uk
www.welltown.gov.uk
www.alcoholconcern.org.uk
www.al-anonuk.org.uk

Alcohol & Other
Drugs Council of
Australia
PO Box 269
Woden ACT 2606
Australia
Tel: 00 621 6281 0686
Email: adca@adca.org.au
Website: www.adca.org.au

Alcohol Drug Association
New Zealand (ADA)
PO Box 13-496
First Floor, 215 Gloucester St
Christchurch, New Zealand
Tel: 03 379 8626
Email: ada@adanz.org.nz
Website: www.adanz.org.nz

There is lots of useful information about alcohol on the internet.

Index

Photocredits

Abbreviations: l-left, r-right, b-bottom, t-top, c-centre, m-middle
All photos supplied by PBD except for:
Front cover, 3br, 5b, 8b, 17b, 23br — Select Pictures. 2, 12, 24r, 25tl, 27b, 28b — Photodisc. 3mr, 7bl,
10b, 20b — Roger Vlitos. 4b — Digital Vision. 7tr — Corel. 11 both, 18b, 19tl — Image State. 13b, 15b,
25br — Corbis. 16r — Flat Earth. 22b — Argentinian Embassy, London. 30b — Brand X Pictures.